Personality Practice of Ministry

A Study in Empirical Theology

Leslie J Francis

Professor of Practical Theology, University of Wales, Bangor

Mandy Robbins

Teaching and Research Fellow
Centre for Ministry Studies, University of Wales, Bangor

GROVE BOOKS LIMITED
RIDLEY HALL RD CAMBRIDGE CB3 9HU

Contents

Foreword

Christian ministry in Britain today is a tough calling. The Pastoral Care Survey was set up to illuminate the challenges and opportunities facing pastors themselves. The initiative came from the Evangelical Alliance and CWR/Waverley Christian Counselling, working in partnership with the Centre for Ministry Studies at the University of Wales, Bangor.

The first study from the Pastoral Care Survey was published in 2000 under the title, *Pastoral Care Today: Practice, Problems and Priorities in Churches Today*. That study concentrated on profiling the pastors' overall responses to the questionnaires which they had completed. This second study, *Personality and the Practice of Ministry*, returns to the information to address one key question: how useful is personality theory in understanding pastoral care today? In this booklet we explain why we believe that personality theory is able to bring a range of insights useful to the future development of the church's mission and ministry.

The authors wish to express their gratitude to the Evangelical Alliance and CWR/Waverley Christian Counselling for this opportunity for fruitful collaboration in empirical theology, to the many pastors who have taken the trouble to complete the questionnaire, to Sean Gubb for inspiring and co-ordinating the project, and to Susan Thomas for working with us on preparing this report.

Address for Correspondence

Leslie J Francis, Director, Welsh National Centre for Religious Education,
University of Wales, Bangor, Normal Site, Bangor, Gwynedd, LL57 2PX UK
Telephone 01248 382566, Fax 01248 383954, email l.j.francis@bangor.ac.uk

The Cover Illustration is by Peter Ashton

First Impression March 2004
ISSN 0144-171X
ISBN 1 85174 558 0

Personality

1

Theology and Personality

The study of personality is concerned with individual differences. Taking people seriously, observing and understanding their individual differences, stands at the very heart of a deeply Christian respect for the rich variety which God the creator built into the very essence of being human.

According to the synoptic tradition, Jesus himself was a highly skilled observer of individual differences. Jesus observed and commented on his observations. In so doing Jesus was able to transcend the specific and draw attention to some generalizable individual differences which resonated with his listeners. Take, for example, the passage from Luke 10, which contrasts two sisters.

> A woman named Martha received Jesus into her house. And she had a sister called Mary, who sat at the Lord's feet and listened to his teaching. But Martha was distracted with much serving.

Do you recognize these individual differences between the socially engaged Martha (extravert) and the reflective Mary (introvert)? In this case Jesus refused to side with Martha against Mary. Mary had chosen the behaviour that suited her personality as an introvert. She was not to be criticized for failing to act like an extravert.

Or take the passage from Luke 15, which contrasts two brothers.

> There was a man who had two sons, and the younger of them said to his father, 'Father, give me the share of property that falls to me.' And he divided his living between them.

You know how the story ends. Do you recognize the individual differences between the adventurous younger son (toughminded) and the cautious older son (tenderminded)? In this case Jesus wanted to make it plain that the father accepted and loved them both, although both had let him down in very different ways.

Those who wish to follow in Jesus' footsteps will continue observing, respecting and accepting individual differences.

Psychology and Personality

Personality psychology, which is concerned with the science of individual differences, has its roots in two very different branches of psychology. On the one hand, depth psychology, as characterized by pioneering names like Sigmund Freud and Carl Gustav Jung, has offered important language and theories for discussing individual differences based on clinical experience. On the other hand, social psychology has offered broader, more empirically grounded concepts and theories based on large population studies. This report is grounded in the second of these two traditions.

The kind of personality theories advanced and discussed by social psychologists are characterized by a finite number of personality factors and self-completion questionnaires constructed to measure these factors. No one theory can really claim to say all there is to say about individual differences. Moreover, these theories do not set out to restrict individuality.

The way to test such personality theories is to see whether or not they work. Commercial airlines make good use of personality theory in recruiting and training pilots. Personality theory helps them to predict who will make safe pilots and who will not. Aeroplanes are expensive to replace and passengers are irreplaceable. This may mean that some people are denied the opportunity to fly jumbo jets on the basis of their personality. Passengers can be quite grateful for that.

Churches may be much more uncertain than commercial airlines about using personality tests to recruit and train clergy. Surely, it can be argued, the God who calls is also faithful to equip for ministry. On the other hand, can churches refuse to make use of the best science available in the service of God? Suppose personality theory could help to identify the priest paedophile? Suppose personality theory could help to identify the pastor who abuses his authority over women, or who misappropriates church resources? Suppose personality theory could help to identify which pastorates are going to flourish under which pastor? Suppose personality theory could help to identify in which posts individual clergy will flourish and which posts will drive them to breakdown? Is it responsible to give the pilot's licence to those who will not make safe landings?

Models of Personality

There is considerable debate among social psychologists regarding the number and nature of the personality factors which it is most useful to employ. Four main theories have attracted most attention. They speak respectively in terms of 16, 5, 4, and 3 main personality factors.

Raymond Cattell, in the United States of America, promoted the 16PF as a model of personality which concentrates on 16 primary or lower order personality factors.[1] This model of personality has been used in a number of studies among clergy in the United States of America and was made known in the United Kingdom through the Edward King Institute. Currently Dr David Musson is publishing valuable research on this model of personality among Anglican clergy in England.[2]

A great deal of international research in the past 15 years has concentrated on exploring the five-factor model of personality.[3] The 'big five' factors of personality have been styled extraversion, agreeableness, conscientiousness, emotional stability, and openness to experience. This model has not yet been used in studies among clergy in the United Kingdom.

Possibly the best known model of personality in church-related circles is the one offered by the Myers-Briggs Type Indicator (MBTI).[4] This model talks in terms of four personality factors, each of which distinguishes between two psychological types. In terms of orientation the model distinguishes between extraversion and introversion. In terms of the perceiving process the model distinguishes between sensing and intuition. In terms of the judging process the model distinguishes between thinking and feeling. In terms of attitude toward the outer world the model distinguishes between perceiving and judging. This model is used quite widely in clergy training, and in some recent research among clergy.[5]

The model which has been most extensively used in research among clergy in the United Kingdom is the one proposed by Hans Eysenck and his associates.[6] In its current form Eysenck's model speaks in terms of the three higher order factors of extraversion, neuroticism, and psychoticism. Over the past decade, we at Bangor have employed this model of personality in a series of studies among Anglican,[7] Methodist,[8] Roman Catholic,[9] and Pentecostal[10] clergy. The present study builds on this foundation, since the earlier studies have clearly demonstrated how Eysenck's model can contribute both to the theory and to the practice of ministry.

Three Dimensions of Personality

Eysenck's three dimensional model of personality has its roots in a theoretical position and in a mathematical observation. The theoretical position understands mental disorder to be continuous with normal personality, not discrete from it. In other words, the individual diagnosed with neurotic disorder is not categorically different from a normal stable individual, but at one extreme end of a personality continuum. This continuum is defined by extreme stability at one end, through emotional liability and anxiety, to neurotic disorder at the opposite end. Similarly, the individual diagnosed with psychotic disorder is not categorically different from a normal tenderminded individual, but at one extreme end of a personality continuum. This continuum is defined by tenderminded well-socialized attitudes at one end, through toughminded antisocial attitudes, to psychotic disorder at the opposite end. In this way Eysenck is able to borrow language from abnormal psychology to describe normal human characteristics.

To describe people, therefore, as scoring high on Eysenck's dimension of neuroticism is not to be saying that they are diagnosed as suffering from neurotic disorder. Similarly, to describe people as scoring high on Eysenck's dimension of psychoticism is not to be saying that they are diagnosed as suffering from psychotic disorder. To the unwary, Eysenck's language may be misleading. It is, nonetheless, a very insightful way of talking about individual differences.

> *To the unwary, Eysenck's language may be misleading, but it is a very insightful way of talking about individual differences*

Eysenck's mathematical position sets out to examine the relationship between individual differences and to suggest mathematically the most economical and efficient way of summarizing these differences. His tool in this mathematical quest was factor analysis. The solution proposed is the three factor model. At the high scoring end these three dimensions are defined as extraversion, neuroticism, and psychoticism. These three dimensions are totally independent of each other. In other words, knowing an individual's position on one of the dimensions does not help to predict his or her position on the other two dimensions. Individuals can score high on one of the dimensions and low on the other two, or in any other combination.

Someone who scores low on neuroticism, low on psychoticism, and high on extraversion would be characterized as a 'stable tenderminded extravert.' Someone who scores high on neuroticism, high on psychoticism, and low on extraversion would be characterized as a 'neurotic toughminded introvert.' Others may score in the middle range of the indices.

The way in which Eysenck's dimensional model of personality is put to work is through one of a series of Eysenck's personality questionnaires. The version used in the present study is the 48-item short-form Revised Eysenck Personality Questionnaire, first published in 1985.[11] This version contains three 12-item scales of extraversion, neuroticism, and psychoticism. There is also a 12-item lie scale to help identify those individuals who wish to present themselves in a particularly favourable light.

Defining the Dimensions

Some of the best and most recent definitions of extraversion, neuroticism, and psychoticism are presented in the manual to the Eysenck Personality Scales published in 1991.[12] The extravert is described in this manual as someone who is:

> sociable, likes parties, has many friends, needs to have people to talk to, and does not like reading or studying by himself. He craves excitement, takes chances, often sticks his neck out, acts on the spur of the moment, and is generally an impulsive individual. He is fond of practical jokes, always has a ready answer, and generally likes change; he is carefree, easy-going, optimistic, and likes to 'laugh and be merry.' He prefers to keep moving and doing things.

By way of contrast, the introvert is described as someone who is:

> a quiet, retiring sort of person, introspective, fond of books rather than people; he is reserved and distant except to intimate friends. He tends to plan ahead, 'looks before he leaps,' and distrusts the impulse of the moment. He does not like excitement, takes matters of everyday life with proper seriousness, and likes a well-ordered mode of life.

The person who records high scores on the neuroticism scale is described as:

> an anxious, worrying individual, moody and frequently depressed. He is likely to sleep badly, and to suffer from various psychosomatic disorders. He is overly emotional, reacting too strongly to all sorts of stimuli, and finds it difficult to get back on an even keel after each emotionally arousing experience. His strong emotional reactions interfere with his proper adjustment, making him react in irrational, sometimes rigid ways.

By way of contrast, the person who records low scores on the neuroticism scale is described as someone who:

> tends to respond emotionally only slowly and generally weakly, and to return to baseline quickly after emotional arousal; he is usually calm, even-tempered, controlled and unworried.

The person who records high scores on the psychoticism scale is described as someone who:

may be cruel and inhumane, lacking in feeling and empathy, and altogether insensitive. He is hostile to others, even his own kith and kin, and aggressive, even to loved ones. He has a liking for odd and unusual things, and a disregard for danger; he likes to make fools of other people, and to upset them. Socialization is a concept which is relatively alien to high P scorers; empathy, feelings of guilt, and sensitivity to other people are notions which are strange and unfamiliar to them.

By way of contrast, the person who records low scores on the psychoticism scale is described as someone who is empathic, unselfish, altruistic, warm, peaceful, and generally more pleasant, although possibly less socially decisive.

2

Pastoral Care Survey

Introduction

In the gospels, Jesus appointed the original twelve disciples to share in his ministry. The disciples were sent out to heal, to teach, and to bring wholeness to others. In this model of pastoral care, the eyes of the blind were opened, the hungry were fed, the poor were upheld, and sinners were brought to repentance. The needs of individuals were identified and responded to.

According to Mark 6.30, the needs of the young trainee pastors were also taken into account. After Jesus had exposed the twelve disciples to their first experience of pastoral work, having sent them out two by two, he gave time to caring for them.

The apostles returned to Jesus, and told him all that they had done and taught. And he said to them, 'Come away by yourselves to a lonely place, and rest a while.' For many were coming and going, and they had no leisure even to eat. And they went away in the boat to a lonely place by themselves.

The Pastoral Care Survey was set up to help the churches reflect on their current practice, to anticipate future trends, and to be better equipped to fulfil their Lord's commission. In addressing these aims, the Pastoral Care Survey envisaged two main approaches. The first approach was to be concerned with using the findings from the survey in a descriptive way to profile current practice, problems, and priorities. The second approach was to employ personality theory to test how this theory could generate fresh insights into pastoral care issues. The first report from the project concentrated on the first approach.[13] The present booklet concentrates on the second approach.

Personality theory was to be employed to test how it could generate fresh insights into pastoral care issues

Personality and Pastoral Care

Alongside all the other questions, the Pastoral Care Today survey included the 48-item Revised Eysenck Personality Questionnaire, first published in 1985. This instrument provides three 12-item indices of extraversion, neuroticism, and psychoticism. It also includes the Eysenck 12-item lie scale. Each item is answered on a simple two point scale: yes and no.

The Eysenck dimensional model of personality was selected in light of the amount of other research in the United Kingdom which is already building up a body of knowledge about clergy personality and in view of the fact that it is a relatively straightforward instrument to administer within the context of a wider questionnaire.

The present analysis uses the information from the short-form Revised Eysenck Personality Questionnaire alongside other data provided by the survey to address four key questions regarding the relationship between personality and pastoral care.

1 Denominational Profiles
The survey included pastors from a number of different denominations. Do different denominations attract into ministry people with significantly different personality profiles?

2 Personality and Membership
Clearly some pastors seem more able than others to lead larger churches. In particular, some pastors seem more able than others to recruit a higher proportion of men into membership. Is there a personality profile associated with such capabilities?

3 Personality and Ministry

Pastors in the survey revealed considerable variations in the weight which they gave to different aspects of ministry, like preaching and visiting. Are there personality profiles associated with valuing specific aspects of ministry? Would personality testing be able to help locate pastors in specific pastorates which would benefit most from their ministry preferences and skills?

4 Personality and Wellbeing

Pastors in the survey reported separately on their physical, mental, and spiritual health, on their satisfaction with ministry, and on their practices of self care. Is there a personality profile associated with wellbeing? Can personality testing help to predict those most vulnerable to poor health?

Conducting the Research

The Pastoral Care Survey was set up among a well-defined group of clergy and pastors. The sample was defined as those clergy and pastors affiliated with the Evangelical Alliance[14] and identified by the Evangelical Alliance mailing list.

This definition of the sample provides both the strength and weakness of the survey. The strength is that the sample is clearly defined. The results provide an authoritative profile of clergy and pastors affiliated with the Evangelical Alliance. The weakness is that the results cannot be generalized to *all* churches. The authors' judgment is that the strength far outweighs the weakness. It is better for good research to be able to speak with authority on a well-defined sample than to claim to make generalizations on the basis of a poorly defined group. Further studies are now needed to extend the present research to other churches.

The questionnaire was designed and tested by consultation between the three sponsors of the study: the Centre for Ministry Studies within the University of Wales, Bangor, the Evangelical Alliance and CWR/Waverley Christian Counselling.

The questionnaire was then mailed to all pastors identified on the Evangelical Alliance mailing list. A total of 2,570 questionnaires were successfully mailed. By the time that the present analysis was initiated, 1,093 thoroughly completed questionnaires had been returned, making a response rate of 43%. In many ways this response rate is disappointingly low. The majority of studies conducted among clergy by the Centre for Ministry Studies have attracted a response rate of over 65% and one reached 82%.[15] Nonetheless, a response rate of 43% allows considerable confidence to be placed in the findings, and especially in the kind of analysis which is looking at relationships between variables rather than trying to establish population levels.

Meeting the Pastors

The first and very striking feature of the pastors who returned their questionnaires was that they were predominantly male: 95% were male and only 5% were female. It may be that women pastors remain under-represented in the Evangelical Alliance constituency. The small number of women in the sample generated a major problem for the planned analysis and with reluctance we excluded them from the subsequent analysis.

Before examining the relationship between personality and specific issues we provide some more detailed description of the 1,037 male pastors who comprise the sample.

Age
Just 1% were under 30, 17% were in their thirties, 37% in their forties, 32% in their fifties and 13% were aged 60 or over. These data demonstrate that the two largest groups of pastors are those in their forties and those in their fifties. The small number of pastors under the age of forty indicates that recruitment into ministry increasingly occurs as a second career after experience in secular employment. The small number of pastors over the age of sixty indicates the pattern of earlier retirement from pastoral responsibility.

Marital Status
Just 2% were single, 1% were widowed, 2% were divorced, and 96% were married. Clearly the norm for pastors affiliated to the Evangelical Alliance is to be married. The low number of divorced pastors raises questions about the churches' pastoral responsibility to pastors who experience marriage break-ups. Many may seem to disappear both from ministry and from the churches' pastoral concern.

Ministry Experience
A third (33%) of them have had less than 10 years in ministry, just over a third (36%) have had between 10 and 19 years in ministry, and just under a third (31%) have had 20 or more years in ministry.

Denomination
The Evangelical Alliance embraces clergy from a wide range of denominational backgrounds. The denominations most strongly represented in the sample are Baptists (28%), Anglicans (19%), the

New Churches (18%), the Pentecostal Churches (10%), the Fellowship of Independent Evangelical Churches (8%), Methodists (4%), Presbyterians and URC (2%) and Congregationalists (1%). The denominations represented by fewer than ten pastors included Brethren and Salvation Army.

Technical Note

This booklet has been written as far as possible to make sense to readers who are unfamiliar with the technical vocabulary and statistical notations of a quantitative approach to personality psychology and empirical theology. At the same time, enough statistical detail has been included on the supporting web page at www.grovebooks.co.uk (under Online Resources) to allow the argument to be properly assessed and evaluated by those with a professional interest in psychology.

Denominational Profiles 3

Previous research on the personality profile of male clergy has drawn attention to two consistent features.

The first feature has emerged through our research among Anglican clergy,[16] Stephen Louden's research among Roman Catholic priests,[17] and John Haley's research among Methodist ministers.[18] In all three of these denominational groups male clergy are found to be significantly more introverted than men in general. Two observations follow from this finding.

First, much of the work which Anglican clergy, Catholic priests, and Methodist ministers are expected to do is work shaped for extraverts. It is extrverts who are energized by standing up in front of people, taking a high profile on public occasions, going out knocking on doors to meet new people, and being publically recognized by others. Introverts are drained and worn down by such experiences. The obvious incompatibility between the nature of the job and the personality of the personnel may help to explain why so many clergy burn out in mid-life and fail to deliver the promise of their vocation.

Second, introversion is classically a prized feminine characteristic, while extraversion is classically a prized masculine characteristic. A lot of the ministry exercised by Anglican clergy, Catholic priests, and Methodist ministers is among women. Introverted clergy tend to feel more at home in that environment. Meanwhile the churches puzzle over the lack of men in the pews. Could it be that many men feel out of place in the kind of environment which the churches have become? Could it be that many men are puzzled by what they observe as the role models of male clergy?

The second feature to have emerged from earlier research on the personality profile of male clergy has been stimulated by William Kay's research among Pentecostal pastors.[19] Pentecostal pastors are different. Pentecostal pastors are significantly more extraverted than their Anglican, Catholic and Methodist colleagues. This means that they present themselves as more active, more sociable, more expressive, more assertive, more achievement orientated, more dogmatic, and more aggressive. In other words, they are more masculine in their approach. I wonder if Pentecostal churches have any more success in attracting men into their congregations?

No previous data have been published on Baptist, Free Evangelical, and New Church pastors.

Personality Factors

Extraversion
The mean extraversion scores for the five denominational groups (table 3.1 on the supporting web page at www.grovebooks.co.uk) confirm that there is a significant difference in the levels of extraversion displayed by pastors associated with different denominations. Anglican and Baptist pastors are less extraverted than Free Evangelical and Pentecostal pastors. New Church pastors are the most extraverted of all. This means that we would expect a more introverted style of ministry in Anglican and Baptist churches and a more extraverted style of ministry in New Church churches.

Neuroticism
The mean neuroticism scores for the five denominational groups (table 3.2) demonstrate that there is a significant difference in the levels of neuroticism displayed by pastors associated with different denominations. This time the distinction is between Pentecostal, Free Evangelical, and New Church pastors scoring lower on the neuroticism scale in comparison with Anglican and Baptist pastors.

Read alongside the significant differences in extraversion scores, these significant differences in neuroticism scores are of particular interest. It is the Baptist and Anglican clergy who are characterized by low extraversion and by high neuroticism in comparison with the other three groups of clergy. Not only are low extraversion scores typically construed as a characteristically feminine personality trait, but high neuroticism scores are also typically construed as a characteristically feminine personality trait. In this sense the Baptist Church now has more in common with Anglicanism than with the Free Evangelical Churches, the New Churches, or the Pentecostal Churches.

Psychoticism
The mean psychoticism scores for the five denominational groups (table 3.3) fail to find any significant differences between Anglican, Baptist, Free Evangelical, New Church, and Pentecostal pastors in terms of psychoticism scores. This finding suggests that the two personality dimensions fundamental to exploring and explaining individual differences in the profile of pastors across denominational groups are extraversion and neuroticism, while such differences remain independent of psychoticism.

This finding is consistent with a completely different strand of research concerned to identify the relationship between Eysenck's dimensional model of personality and religiosity more generally.[20] This strand of research has concluded that neither extraversion scores nor neuroticism scores help to predict levels of religiosity, while religious people overall consistently record lower scores on the psychoticism scale than people who are not religious. It seems, therefore, that while psychoticism is fundamental to the difference between religious people and irreligious people, extraversion and neuroticism may be fundamental to the ways in which religious people express their religion.

Charismatic Movement

Another way of conceptualizing denominational differences concerns the influence of the charismatic movement. A series of studies conducted by Hugh Thomas[21] and James Hair[22] among Anglican clergy and by Stephen Louden[23] among Catholic priests have established a clear link between extraversion and attraction toward the charismatic movement. In both denominations introverted clergy are less likely to be attracted to the charismatic movement. These earlier studies have assessed attraction to the charismatic movement through a series of interrelated questions of which speaking or praying in tongues is one element. These earlier studies have not, however, isolated glossolalia by itself as a focus for analysis.

Within the wider literature in the psychology of religion, the personality dimension of greatest interest in relation to glossolalia is that of neuroticism. A number of early theories in the psychology of religion tried to link glossolalia with various forms of psychopathology associated with neuroticism. Other theoretical positions, however, suggested that glossolalia may function as a tension-reducing device which may promote psychological health. None of the earlier studies published by Hugh Thomas, James Hair, or Stephen Louden found any evidence to associate glossolalia with elevated neuroticism scores, while Hugh Thomas' study actually found lower neuroticism scores among those attracted to the charismatic movement.

The analysis in the present study focuses specifically on the relationship between personality and the reported frequence of speaking in tongues (glossolalia) which was assessed on a six point scale: nearly every day, at least once a week, at least once a month, occasionally, used to but not now, and never. The statistics (table 3.4) show that frequency of glossolalia is associated with higher extraversion scores and with lower neuroticism scores, but independent of psychoticism. These findings confirm the view that introverted clergy are less likely to be glossolalic. They also demonstrate that the clergy who practise glossolalia are more psychologically stable than clergy who do not practice glossolalia. Glossolalia is associated with good mental health, not with psychopathology. Early theories in the psychology of religion which saw glossolalia as pathological clearly got it wrong.

4 Personality and Membership

Introduction

It is clear from casual observation and anecdote that some pastors build up larger and stronger churches than others. 'So much,' it is often said, 'is down to the pastor's personality.' In this colloquial sense personality is being used to suggest little more than the fact that some pastors seem to attract more success than others. But what can be learnt by setting church size against a scientifically constructed personality profile?

Membership

Intuition might suggest that extraverted pastors are better equipped than introverted pastors to build up membership and attendance. After all, much of church growth is predicated on human interaction and personal relationships, and extraverts are known to be better and quicker at establishing relationships in comparison with introverts. Also stable pastors are better equipped than neurotic pastors to build up membership and attendance. After all, much of successful ministry is predicated on not upsetting people and on refusing to be hurt by others' reactions, and neurotic individuals are known to be more easily offended and to give offence more readily.

The following analysis, therefore, focuses on the relationship between personality and two aspects of church size: the number of members; and the proportion of members who are male.

Members

The statistics (table 4.1) confirm the view that larger numbers of members are associated with pastors who score high on the extraversion scale and low on the neuroticism scale. Taking these two dimensions of personality together, the largest memberships are within the care of stable extraverted pastors, while the smallest memberships are within the hands of neurotic introverted pastors.

Men and women

The second question on church size in the Pastoral Care Survey asked the pastors to report the percentages of their membership who were male and who were female. The statistics (table 4.2) demonstrate that the more extraverted clergy are likely to attract a higher proportion of men into membership. This finding is consistent with the views that extraversion is classically a masculine characteristic and that men are more likely to be attracted to churches in which the pastor projects a more masculine personality profile.

Induction Programmes

Induction programmes may play an important part in patterns of church membership. Churches clearly treat new attenders in a variety of different ways. Some churches take a very casual approach and leave new attenders to make their own way into fellowship and into membership. Other churches take a much more proactive view of how new attenders should be approached.

The strategy adopted by the local church may have a lot to do with the church's theological understanding of the nature of its mission. But is there also a sense in which the pastor is projecting his or her own personality onto the expectations of new attenders?

Once again the key personality dimension at stake is likely to be extraversion. Beginning to attend a new church is a very significant step in the world of social interaction. Extraverts who attend a church for the first time may long to be engaged in conversation, to be introduced to church members, and to find themselves immediately linked into a pastoral programme. Introverts who attend a church for the first time may long to slip in unnoticed, dread the thought of being engaged in conversation, and hope to avoid the intimidation of pastoral programmes. What in fact new attenders find may depend to some extent on what the pastor would want to find, were he or she in their shoes.

In order to test this kind of theory the Pastoral Care Survey asked pastors to identify which pastoral care programmes they had for new attenders by checking a list. The data (table 4.3) indicated that psychoticism scores were completely irrelevant for shaping their provision and neuroticism scores were almost completely irrelevant. Extraversion scores, however, had a significant part to play. The statistics show that extravert pastors were more likely to follow-up new attenders with a visit and telephone calls. They were more likely to offer an induction programme to church life and to provide a link with other church members. They were more likely to try to locate new members in a home group and to provide them with introductory literature. All of these strategies are well designed to draw their fellow extraverts into a rewarding relationship with the church. The downside, however, is that these self same strategies may well drive introvert enquirers straight back into their homes. Clearly pastors need to be aware of how their preferred styles of ministry will affect different types of people

5 Personality and Ministry

Introduction

Since the classic studies by Blizzard in the 1950s[24] there has been a strand of research concerned with describing and defining the various roles associated with Christian ministry. No one commonly agreed list of roles has emerged, although there are some key roles which appear to be common to most lists, like preacher and worship leader.

Role Priorities

What is clear from casual observation is that some clergy seem to give a high priority to a specific role while other clergy give a low priority to the same role. Some of these individual differences in role prioritization may be attributable to different theological positions or to different church traditions. Within Anglicanism the clergy who espouse an anglo-catholic tradition will give greater weight to a sacramental ministry than is the case among the clergy who espouse an evangelical tradition. Some of these individual differences in role prioritization will simply be attributable to personal taste. But how much does basic personality contribute to such differences in role prioritization?

In the early 1990s Raymond Rodger[25] asked the question about the relationship between personality and role prioritization among a sample of Anglican clergymen in the Diocese of Lincoln. His data provided evidence for precisely such an association. Raymond Rodger's findings were subsequently replicated by Mandy Robbins in a survey among Anglican clergywomen.[26]

The present analysis focuses on the role inventory included in the Pastoral Care Survey. The pastors were asked to rate the priority which they want to give in their ministry to each of 20 identified roles: administrator, apostle, counsellor, evangelist, fellowship-builder, fund-raiser, leader in the local community, leader of public worship, man or woman of prayer, manager, minister of sacraments, pastor, pioneer, preacher, prophet, social worker, spiritual director, teacher, theologian and visitor. They were asked to rate the priority which they wanted to give to each of these aspects of ministry on a seven point scale, from very little to very much. Since a number of correlations are being considered simultaneously in this section, only those which reach the one percent level will be interpreted.

Extraversion

Nine roles were rated more highly by extraverts than by introverts (table 5.1). The extravert pastors are more likely to see their ministry in terms of being a pioneer, being a leader in the community, being an evangelist, and being an apostle. They are also more likely to see their ministry in terms of being a prophet, a fund-raiser, a fellowship-builder, and a social worker. All of these ministry roles are consistent with being the type of person who likes to be busily involved with people. Churches which wish to encourage their pastors to emphasize these kinds of roles might be well advised to appoint someone who scores high on the extraversion scale. Pastors who score low on the extraversion scale may struggle to fulfil such expectations.

Neuroticism

Three roles were rated more highly by those scoring high on the neuroticism scale than by those scoring low on this scale (table 5.2). The pastors who score high on the neurotic scale are more likely to see their ministry in terms of being a minister of sacraments, a theologian, or a leader of public worship. All of these ministry roles are consistent with being the type of person who likes to be protected by clearly defined functions from the unpredictable pressures of unplanned human interaction. Because their energy is being directed in these areas, the more neurotic pastors may make very fine ministers of the sacraments, theologians, and leaders of public worship. Churches which wish to encourage their pastors to emphasize these kinds of roles might be well advised to appoint someone who scores high on the neuroticism scale. Pastors who score low on the neuroticism scale may lack the drive to excel in such areas.

The more neurotic pastors may make very fine ministers of the sacraments, theologians, and leaders of public worship

Psychoticism

Three roles were rated more highly by those scoring high on the psychoticism scale than by those scoring low on this scale (table 5.3). The pastors who score high on the psychoticism scale are more likely to see their ministry in terms of being a pioneer, an apostle, and an evangelist. These three roles also appear higher in the list of extravert pastors, but in that case these three roles are part of a wider set of roles symbolizing human interaction. For the pastor who scores high on the psychoticism scale, these three roles in isolation may mean something rather different from what they mean to the extravert. They may symbolize a way of doing things *to* people rather than doing things *with* and *for* them.

Churches may need to be careful not to be misled by the way in which pastors who score high on the psychoticism scale may tend to disguise their loner tendencies by using benign religious language. In the mouths of those who score high on extraversion, words like pioneer and evangelist signal a desire to shape a community. In the mouths of those who score high on psychoticism, the self same words may signal a desire to manipulate and to control others.

While only high scorers on the extraversion scale and high scorers on the neuroticism scale identified distinctive emphases in the role prioritization, in the case of the psychoticism scale low scorers as well as high scorers revealed distinctive emphases in role prioritization (table 5.4).

The pastors who score low on the psychoticism scale are more likely to see their ministry in terms of being a pastor, a visitor, a fellowship-builder, and a teacher. All of these ministry roles are consistent with being the type of person who likes to be gently caring for others. These are the ministry roles adopted by pastors for whom other people really matter. Churches which wish to encourage their pastors to emphasize these kinds of roles might be well advised to appoint someone who scores low on the psychoticism scale.

Collaborative Ministry

Many denominations talk in terms of encouraging collaborative ministry in one form or another. In some cases, the move to collaborative ministry is theologically driven, as churches speak in terms of all-member ministry and in terms of baptism equipping for ministry. In other cases, the move to collaborative ministry is driven by practical concerns to do with shortage of finance, the lack of trained pastors, or the enormity of the task to be done.

Whatever individual pastors say about their commitment to collaborative ministry, it seems clear that some find it easier than others to implement a shared style of ministry. To what extent does basic personality play a part in shaping their response?

In order to address this question, the Pastoral Care Survey invited pastors to assess the proportion of pastoral care in their churches which was provided by other people. Alongside the professional salaried colleagues, the survey listed four categories of volunteers: members of the congregation; counsellors; elders; and home group leaders. The proportion of pastoral care provided by each of these four categories was assessed on a seven point scale, from very little to very much. The pastor's psychoticism scores were unrelated to the proportion of pastoral care carried out by these people. Extraversion scores and neuroticism scores were, however, both significant predictors.

Extravert pastors see a higher proportion of pastoral care being carried out by elders, by counsellors, and by home group leaders, in comparison with introvert pastors (see table 5.5). This suggests that extravert pastors are happier than introvert pastors in involving others alongside them in collaborative ministry. This observation is consistent with the view that extraverts generally enjoy working with other people, while introverts may often prefer working by themselves.

Extravert pastors see a higher proportion of pastoral care being carried out by elders, counsellors and home group leaders

Stable pastors see a higher proportion of pastoral care being carried out by elders, by house group leaders, by members of the congregation, and by counsellors, in comparison with pastors who record higher scores on the neuroticism scale (see table 5.6). This suggests that pastors who display a more stable personality are happier than pastors who display a more neurotic personality in involving others alongside them in collaborative ministry. This observation is consistent with the view that individuals who record high scores on the neuroticism scale generally experience greater hesitation and difficulty in trusting and working with others.

Churches which wish to make good use of collaborative ministry and to promote effective deployment of ministry teams might be well advised to appoint a stable extravert as pastor. Churches which expect the pastor to work unsupported by collaborative ministry or ministry teams might well find that the stable extravert pastor is less suited to that way of working.

6   Personality and Wellbeing

Introduction

There is now a lot of evidence in the psychological literature to link personality with both physical and psychological wellbeing. For example, one recent set of studies we conducted has explored the relationship between personality and happiness among students in the United Kingdom,[27] United States of America,[28] Germany,[29] and Israel.[30] In all of these samples happiness was associated with stable extraversion and largely independent of psychoticism. This chapter concentrates on three main aspects of wellbeing among the clergy: general health; dissatisfaction with ministry; and self-care.

General health

The section on the relationship between personality and general health looked at three specific issues—physical health, mental health, and spiritual health. Each aspect of health was rated independently on a five point scale of excellent, good, middling, poor and very poor. The statistics (tables 6.1, 6.2, and 6.3) show that good physical health, good mental health and good spiritual health are all associated with stable extraversion, while poor physical health, poor mental health and poor spiritual health are all associated with neurotic introversion.

This kind of information from personality psychology could be used creatively to identify those pastors most likely to be at risk from experiencing poor health, physically, mentally, or spiritually. Once identified, additional support could be provided. Such information might also helpfully influence decisions on where individual pastors could be most satisfactorily deployed, taking into account the type of health-related support they may need and the ways in which different pastorates are variously equipped to provide such help.

Dissatisfaction with Ministry

One of the most startling statistics to emerge from the the Pastoral Care Survey is that over half of the pastors admit that they have considered leaving the ministry. Moreover, this statistic has to be set alongside recognition that the Pastoral Care Survey had been sent only to pastors in active ministry. In other words, the survey did not include those who had already left ministry.

In some senses leaving ministry for other forms of employment may be seen as a very healthy sign against the background of today's society. Today very few jobs are 'for life' and it is increasingly common for people to have more than one job or professional career in their life time. Perhaps it needs to be more accepted that pastors may move in and out of ministry at various stages of their career.

In other senses, however, leaving ministry may be seen in more negative terms. There is evidence to suggest that some of those who leave do so as hurt, disappointed or damaged individuals. This clearly represents bad pastoral care of those who have themselves set out to show pastoral care to others. Standing back and watching pastors leave the ministry may also make less than good sense for the churches. Few denominations appear to be so over blessed with vocations to ministry that they work actively to drive pastors away. Indeed those denominations struggling to afford clergy stipends may prefer to encourage some clergy to move into non-stipendiary ministry, rather than to abandon ministry altogether. Second, since clergy tend to be quite expensive to train, it may not make good economic sense to fail to care for them after they have been trained.

Earlier research by Raymond Rodger[31] suggested that personality theory can help to predict those clergy most likely to entertain thoughts of leaving ministry. The aim of the following analysis, therefore, is to focus on the relationship between personality and thoughts of leaving ministry. The clergy were asked to respond to the question, 'Have you, since ordination, ever considered leaving the ministry?' on a four point scale—frequently, several times, once or twice, and no.

The statistics (table 6.4) show that thoughts of leaving ministry are positively associated with neuroticism, but independent of extraversion and psychoticism. Taking neuroticism scores seriously may help church leaders to predict those clergy most likely to exit prematurely from ministry.

Self-care

Pastors who provide the pastoral care for others themselves deserve to be in receipt of pastoral care. It is clear from the Pastoral Care Survey that pastors differ considerably among themselves in terms of the pastoral care which they need and the pastoral care which they permit themselves to receive. This final section in the present booklet examines the relationship between personality and individual differences in the pastoral care which clergy need and in the pastoral care which they permit themselves to receive.

In order to provide a sharp focus to this section, attention is given to three specific issues: exhaustion; benefit derived from in-service training; and the receipt of pastoral care.

Exhaustion

The Pastoral Care Survey included the very telling statement, 'I feel over-whelmed by pastoral care demands.' Nearly two-fifths (38%) of the pastors said 'yes' to this question. The statistics (table 6.5) make it clear that the feeling of being overwhelmed or exhausted by the demands of pastoral responsi-bilities is independent of both extraversion and psychoticism, but significantly related to neuroticism. Pastors who record high scores on the neuroticism scale are more likely to feel overwhelmed by their ministry than pastors who score low on this scale.

Given the way in which exhaustion can become disfunctional for the pastor and debilitating for the church, there may be considerable advantage in iden-tifying the pastors most likely to suffer in this way. Pastoral care which intervenes before it is too late can be beneficial to the individual pastor and to the local church. Personality testing appears to be helpful in predicting such tendencies.

In-service Training

In theory, in-service training can provide a crucial means of support and encouragement for pastors. The Pastoral Care Survey included a statement about the beneficial influence derived from in-service training on the pas-tors' understanding of pastoral care. They were invited to rate this issue on a seven point scale, from very little to very much. Clearly some had found in-service training beneficial and some had not.

The statistics (table 6.6) make it clear that there is a positive association between extraversion and valuing in-service training, a negative association between neuroticism and valuing in-service training, and a negative asso-ciation between psychoticism and valuing in-service training. In other words, those who derive most benefit from in-service training are tenderminded stable extraverts, while those who derive least benefit from in-service train-ing are the toughminded neurotic introverts.

It is ironic that the pastors who score high on the neuroticism scale feel both more exhausted by delivering pastoral care and also less able to receive benefit from in-service training. The best way to help these people deal with their exhaustion may not, therefore, simply be through providing more in-service training programmes for them. If this is the case, there are implications both for those who provide in-service training and for those who stand to benefit from such provisions.

Trainers will recognize the need to target different programmes for different types of pastors. While the stable extravert pastor may well be resourced and re-energized by group events, the neurotic introvert pastor may be resourced and refreshed more effectively by individual and personal pursuits. Pastors will recognize how their own particular training needs can best be shaped in response to who they are. One provision simply does not fit all shapes and sizes, and should never be expected to do so.

Conclusion 7

This booklet has drawn on a recent survey conducted among clergy from several different denominations in order to test the usefulness of personality theory for understanding and improving pastoral care today.

As a study in empirical theology it has examined the evidence. Three main conclusions can be drawn and two practical recommendations can be formulated on the basis of existing research in this area.

The **first conclusion** is that different personality profiles equip individual pastors to exercise ministry in distinctive and predictable ways. Certain expectations of ministry, for example, are fulfilled most adequately by stable extraverts. Locating neurotic introverts into such posts runs the risk of disappointing the congregations which hold such expectations and harming the health of the pastor. There are other equally valuable areas of ministry in which the neurotic introvert would excel and where the stable extravert would experience and generate disappointment. The God who creates diversity in personality may also rejoice in diversity in ministry.

The **second conclusion** is that some personality profiles are associated with higher risks of exhaustion, burnout, and ill-health in ministry. Churches properly select such candidates into ministry, recognizing the divine call to vocation across the diversity of human personality. Churches which recruit, train and ordain such candidates may nonetheless need to remain committed to providing appropriate support at those points when the strains of ministry take their toll.

The **third conclusion** is that the criteria of selection across the denominations varies in subtle ways which may well reflect covert bias and hidden assumptions regarding the indicators of divine calling and of mature spirituality. For example, among Anglicans such indicators are more likely to be discerned in the depth of introverted faith, while among the Pentecostal Churches such indicators are more likely to be discerned in the exuberance of extraverted faith.

The **first recommendation** is that church leaders, church managers, and church educators should be encouraged to make better use of personality theory in the processes of selecting, training and developing pastors. It makes good sense to identify the qualities required in different areas of ministry and to select and appoint candidates whose personality equips them to exercise such qualities. Taking the personality of pastors seriously should bring benefits to the physical, mental, and spiritual health of the pastors themselves. As a consequence it should also bring benefits to the effective mission of the church which those pastors are called and equipped to serve.

The insights of personality theory should be made more routinely available to pastors themselves

The **second recommendation** is that the insights of personality theory should be made more routinely available to pastors themselves both during their initial training and during their continuing professional development. Taking personality theory seriously should enhance their awareness of the subtle power of their own personality preferences to influence their approach to pastoral care issues. It should also enhance self-awareness of their personal strengths and vulnerabilities in the service of their Lord. Pastors blessed with the hidden depths of introversion have no reason to berate themselves for failing to create the vibrant community that extraverts achieve so naturally. Pastors blessed with the visible social skills of extraversion have no reason to berate themselves for failing to develop the quiet meditative spirituality that introverts achieve so naturally. Both are called to rejoice in the diverse gifts with which the creator God has endowed them so magnificently.

Notes

1   R B Cattell, H E Eber and M M Tatsuoka, *Handbook for the Sixteen Personality Factor Questionnaire (16PF)* (Champaign, Illinois: IPAT, 1970).

2   D J Musson, 'The Personality Profile of Male Anglican Clergy in England: The 16PF' *Personality and Individual Differences*, 1998, 25, pp 689-698; L J Francis and D J Musson, 'Male and Female Anglican Clergy in England: Gender reversal on the 16PF?' *Journal of Empirical Theology*, 1999, 12(2), pp 5-16; D J Musson, 'Male and Female Anglican Clergy: Gender reversal on the 16PF5?' *Review of Religious Research*, 2001, 43, pp 175-183; D J Musson and L J Francis, 'A Comparison of the Psychometric Properties of the 16PF4 and 16PF5 Among Male Anglican Clergy' *Pastoral Psychology*, 2002, 50, pp 281-289; D J Musson, 'Personality of Male Anglican Clergy in England: Revisited using the 16PF5' *Mental Health, Religion and Culture*, 2002, 5, pp 195-206.

3   P T Costa (jr) and R R McCrae, *The NEO Personality Inventory Manual* (Odessa, Florida: Psychological Assessment Resources, 1985).

4   I B Myers and M H McCaulley, *Manual: a guide to the development and use of the Myers-Briggs Type Indicator* (Palo Alto, California: Consulting Psychologists Press, 1985).

5   L J Francis, V J Payne and S H Jones, 'Psychological Types of Male Anglican Clergy in Wales,' *Journal of Psychological Type*, 2001, 56, pp 19-23; L J Francis, A W Penson and S H Jones, 'Psychological Types of Male and Female Bible College Students in England,' *Mental Health, Religion and Culture*, 2001, 4, pp 23-32.

6   H J Eysenck and M W Eysenck, *Personality and Individual Differences: A natural science approach* (New York: Plenum Press, 1985).

7   L J Francis, 'The Personality Characteristics of Anglican Ordinands: Feminine men and masculine women?' *Personality and Individual Differences*, 1991, 12, pp 1133-1140; L J Francis and R Rodger, 'The Personality Profile of Anglican Clergymen,' *Contact*, 1994, 113, pp 27-32; M Robbins, J Hair and L J Francis, 'Personality and Attraction to the Charismatic Movement: A study among Anglican clergy,' *Journal of Beliefs and Values*, 1999, 20, pp 239-246; M Robbins, L J Francis and W Fletcher-Marsh, 'Personality Profile of Anglican Clergywomen in Canada and England: A cross cultural comparison on the EPQR-S,' *Pastoral Sciences*, 2000, 19, pp 79-90.

8   M Robbins, L J Francis, J M Haley and W K Kay, 'The Personality Characteristics of Methodist Ministers: Feminine men and masculine women?' *Journal for the Scientific Study of Religion*, 2001, 40, pp 123-128.

9   S H Louden and L J Francis, 'The Personality Profile of Roman Catholic Parochial Secular Priests in England and Wales,' *Review of Religious Research*, 1999, 41, pp 65-79; L J Francis and S H Louden, 'Mystical Orientation and Psychological Type: A study among student and adult churchgoers,' *Transpersonal Psychology Review*, 2000, 4 (1), pp 36-42; S H Louden and L J Francis, 'Are Catholic Priests in England and Wales Attracted to the Charismatic Movement Emotionally Less Stable?' *British Journal of Theological Education*, 2001, 11, pp 65-76; L J Francis and S H Louden, 'Parish Ministry and Roman Catholic Regular Clergy: Applying Eysenck's dimensional model of personality,' *International Journal of Practical Theology*, 2001, 5, pp 216-226.

10 L J Francis and W K Kay, 'The Personality Characteristics of Pentecostal Ministry Candidates,' *Personality and Individual Differences*, 1995, 18, pp 581-594; W K Kay, *Pentecostals in Britain* (Carlisle: Paternoster, 2000).

11 S B G Eysenck, H J Eysenck and P Barrett, 'A Revised Version of the Psychoticism Scale,' *Personality and Individual Differences*, 1985, 6, pp 21-29.

12 H J Eysenck and S B G Eysenck, *Manual of the Eysenck Personality Scales* (London: Hodder and Stoughton, 1991).

13 L J Francis, M Robbins and W K Kay, *Pastoral Care Today: Practice, problems and priorities in churches today* (Farnham: CWR, 2000).

14 I Randall and D Hilborn, *One Body in Christ: The history and significance of the Evangelical Alliance* (Carlisle: Paternoster Press, 2001).

15 S H Jones and L J Francis, 'The Fate of the Welsh Clergy: An attitude survey among male clerics in the Church in Wales,' *Contemporary Wales*, 1997, 10, pp 182-199.

16 L J Francis, 'The Personality Characteristics of Anglican Ordinands: Feminine men and masculine women?' *Personality and Individual Differences*, 1991, 12, pp 1133-1140.

17 S H Louden and L J Francis, 'The Personality Profile of Roman Catholic Parochial Secular Priests in England and Wales,' *Review of Religious Research*, 1999, 41, pp 65-79.

18 M Robbins, L J Francis and W K Kay, 'The Personality Characteristics of Methodist Ministers: Feminine men and masculine women?' *Journal for the Scientific Study of Religion*, 2001, 40, pp 123-128.

19 W K Kay, *Pentecostals in Britain* (Carlisle: Paternoster, 2000).

20 L J Francis, J M Lewis, L B Brown, R Philipchalk and D Lester, 'Personality and Religion Among Undergraduate Students in the United Kingdom, United States, Australia and Canada,' *Journal of Psychology and Christianity*, 1995, 14, pp 250-262.

21 L J Francis and T H Thomas, 'Are Charismatic Ministers Less Stable? A study among male Anglican clergy,' *Review of Religious Research*, 1997, 39, pp 61-69.

22 M Robbins, J Hair and L J Francis, 'Personality and Attraction to the Charismatic Movement: A study among Anglican clergy,' *Journal of Beliefs and Values*, 1999, 20, pp 239-246.

23 S H Louden and L J Francis, 'Are Catholic Priests in England and Wales Attracted to the Charismatic Movement Emotionally Less Stable?' *British Journal of Theological Education*, 2001, 11, pp 65-76.

24 S W Blizzard, 'The Parish Minister's Self-image of his Master Role,' *Pastoral Psychology*, 1958, 89, pp 25-32; S W Blizzard, 'The Protestant Parish Minister's Integrating Roles,' *Religious Education*, 1958, 53, pp 374-380.

25 L J Francis and R Rodger, 'The Influence of Personality on Clergy Role Prioritization, Role Influences, Conflict and Dissatisfaction with Ministry,' *Personality and Individual Differences*, 1994, 16, pp 947-957.

26 M Robbins and L J Francis, 'Role Prioritization Among Clergywomen: The influence of personality and church tradition among female stipendiary Anglican clerics in the UK,' *British Journal of Theological Education*, 2000, 11, pp 7-23.

27 M Robbins and L J Francis, 'Are Religious People Happier? A study among undergraduates' in L J Francis, W K Kay and W S Campbell (eds), *Research in Religious Education* (Leominster: Gracewing, 1996), pp 207-217; L J Francis, S H Jones and C Wilcox, 'Religiosity and Happiness: During adolescence, young adulthood and later life,' *Journal of Psychology and Christianity*, 2000, 19, pp 245-257.

28 L J Francis and D Lester, 'Religion, Personality and Happiness,' *Journal of Contemporary Religion*, 1997, 12, pp 81-86.

29 L J Francis, H-G Ziebertz and C A Lewis, 'The Relationship Between Religion and Happiness Among German Students,' *Pastoral Psychology*, 2003 (in press).

30 L J Francis and Y J Katz, 'Religiosity and Happiness: A study among Israeli female undergraduates,' *Research in the Social Scientific Study of Religion*, 2002, 13, pp 75-86.

31 L J Francis and R Rodger, 'The Influence of Personality on Clergy Role Prioritization, Role Influences, Conflict and Dissatisfaction with Ministry,' *Personality and Individual Differences*, 1994, 16, pp 947-957.